# GOT MELC?

Ryan Kus

A Collaborative Publication of Gold Leaf Press

**got MELC?**
By Ryan Kus

Editorial Director: Rebecca J. Ensign
Book and Cover Design: Boisvert Design

A Collaborative Publication of Gold Leaf Press
Detroit, MI
www.goldleafpress.com

©2012 Ryan Kus

All rights reserved. No part of this publication may be reproduced, stored in a retrieval system, or transmitted in any way or any form, electronic, mechanical, photocopying, recording or otherwise, without the written permission of the Author.

Library of Congress Control Number: 2012945510

ISBNs
**Print:** 10 digit: 1-886769-72-9
13 digit: 978-1-886769-72-4

**Digital:** Available as a pdf download.
10 digit: 1-886769-73-7
13 digit: 978-1-886769-73-1

64 pages; Soft cover; $7.95

10 9 8 7 6 5 4 3 2 1

Printed in the U.S.A.

# Dedication

This book is dedicated to my daughter, Charley. Growing up in a family where I had lost my mother and sister early in life, I see the need to have memories of family. Life goes by quickly and I believe it is important to leave a footprint that will be remembered for years to come. Having my daughter has inspired me to want to leave a lasting legacy for her. Charley, my love is so deep for you and I hope you have much success in life! Remember to always be nice to people and work hard.

# Acknowledgments

I'd like to thank many individuals who have shaped the work ethic that I have today. I have been fortunate in life to be surrounded by successful business minds and I appreciate all the time and effort they have provided me!

To the agents who work closely with me, you have helped me with all of your ideas and encouragement which I was able to use to create this book.

To Dennis Brown and Tim Otto, who helped me create a stage to help agents across the country, and make sure that we keep teaching.

To Rachel Kus, who allows me to work long hours with a smile on her face. Love you!

**And, to the following three people whose words inspire me every day.**

*"I've had smarter people around me all my life, but I haven't run into one yet that can outwork me. And if they can't outwork you, then smarts aren't going to do them much good. That's just the way it is. And if you believe that and live by it, you'd be surprised at how much fun you can have."* ~ **Woody Hayes**

*"No one has ever drowned in sweat."* ~ **Lou Holtz**

*"There is no substitute for hard work."* ~ **Thomas A. Edison**

# Foreword

*Got MELC?* is a wake-up call to every American who will one day leave a legacy to their family. Ryan Kus is an industry expert and makes many important and valid points that can help improve people's financial positions with taking on little or no risk.

Nobody knows what the future holds, where tax rates will be, and if the stock market will be up or down. By repositioning assets that are earmarked for the next generation, you can make certain that a known amount of money is passed down at an unknown time. Positioning these dollars to be income tax free is an even more important part of the planning process and why it makes even more sense.

I recommend that everyone who has a similar objective read this book and become educated on an innovative advanced estate planning strategy that has been utilized for generations among the super-wealthy.

Alexander Dinser, ChFC

*CERTIFIED FINANCIAL PLANNER* ™

# Contents

**Introduction**  What's MELC? ................................................................ 1

**Chapter 1**  Legacy or Liability? ......................................................... 3

**Chapter 2**  Economic Trends: Do you have blinders on? ............. 7

**Chapter 3**  Is the Family Legacy Important to You? ................... 17

**Chapter 4**  What is Your Exit Strategy? ......................................... 23

**Chapter 5**  Can You Relate to This? ............................................... 33

**Chapter 6**  Can You Maximize Your Legacy? ............................... 39

**Conclusion**  ........................................................................................ 43

**Glossary of Key Terms** ..................................................................... 45

# Introduction
## What's MELC?

It has been projected that $11.6 trillion in inter-generational wealth is, or will be, transferred in the U.S., including some $2.4 trillion that has already been gifted.

In fact, two out of three baby boomers – those who were born from 1943-1960 – should get something; most can expect to enjoy a median inheritance amount of $64,000, before taxes. [Source: "Inheritance and Wealth Transfer to Baby Boomers"; Commissioned by MetLife from Boston College's Center for Retirement Research]

This means that there are a lot of parents going through their daily lives with a sense of a financial legacy and a lot of "kids" going through their daily lives with a sense of financial promise. Yet many of them are doing so completely unaware of the ensuing financial crisis they are either creating or about to encounter as a result of their ill-informed expectations.

When you think about it, money – whether it's earned, won or inherited – has only one "dark side". Taxes! Whenever there's a sad story about someone who came into a whole lot of money, it's usually sad because of the taxes. And while you can't do much about avoiding taxes if you win the lottery or get a huge bonus, you – and your parents – certainly can do something about an inheritance. That's where MELC comes in.

## got MELC?

MELC stands for Maximum Efficiency Life Contract. In this book you will be introduced to how you can use MELC to maximize your legacy or inheritance.

Don't worry if you've never heard of MELC. Not many people have. But this book intends to change that.

Presented to inform the uninformed, alert the unaware and prepare the unprepared, this book speaks out to those who are building a financial legacy and those who will inherit a financial legacy; the goal of which is to be an enhancement, not a detriment for all involved.

This book is not designed to give you all the answers, but it will prompt questions … questions that you need to ask based upon your individual circumstances, preferences and goals for your legacy.

You have choices; there are wise choices and not so wise choices. The most important thing for you to understand is that you are capable of not only making the wisest choices, but also recognizing them on your own. This is done through gathering a little information (by reading this book), then asking the right person the right questions.

# Chapter 1

## Legacy or Liability?

A father has spent a lifetime with one real hope, to help his son financially. He has scrimped, saved, and put off vacations that his family would have preferred to take. He and his wife decided to live frugally in retirement; if not, how would their money last? In fact, nearly every month, he was able to actually save a portion of his pension and social security income. Sadly, his wife passed away much sooner than expected. His one solace during his remaining years was watching his retirement savings grow.

After a while he was sure that he would be able to pass almost all of his retirement savings account on to his beloved son. He was about to do one of the kindest and most loving things a parent can do. Yet, he was also unknowingly putting his son in a compromised position. You see, he had saved all that money in tax qualified accounts, allowing every penny to work for him as it grew over all those years. He had overlooked the fact that not one penny of taxes was paid on any of the savings or the interest that compounded over the years. And his son, whose financial priorities were a bit different than his dad's, was also oblivious to inheritance tax liabilities.

Unlike his dad, the son was much more willing to invest in his family's relaxation. He and his wife had their eyes on a beautiful second home on a marvelous lake several hours from their main home. His inheritance would give them just enough to buy it and pay the closing costs. So, when his father passed away in late January, he and his wife liquidated the IRA and purchased the house. Their dream came true.

Thanks to dad, he and his wife would now be able to spend their summers at their lovely summer home. However, the first April following his dad's death, their American dream became a bit of an Uncle Sam nightmare. Their accountant informed them that they owed a significant sum to the IRS.

The IRA distribution they had inherited that year was added to their ordinary income which instantly raised them into the highest bracket. They had used all of the proceeds to purchase the house. They had nothing left and were about to join the growing number of "accidental inheritance victims."

These are victims of a financial crisis you never hear about; a quiet crisis, a private crisis that silently brews throughout a person's lifetime then attacks with full force in one fell swoop – usually around tax time, when the victim is completely unprepared. And with no quick fix, unless the victim has a great deal of money or liquid assets, it can take a lifetime to resolve.

Notice that we refer to these unfortunate people as "accidental inheritance victims". Sadly, that's exactly what they are; through no fault of their own (accidentally), they are thrust into a severe financial crisis (victimized) as a result of their inheritance. But, does that make their parents or grandparents wicked? Of course not! No loving parent or grandparent would deliberately do this to their kids or grandkids. They simply did not know or understand that the tax liabilities associated with the funds don't go away; the person who inherits those funds also inherits the taxes due for those funds.

This happens to Americans of all ages, from all walks of life, every day in every U.S. city. But, it doesn't have to happen to you regardless of which person you are – the parent striving to build and pass on your financial legacy or the kid who will receive it.

Given these facts, legacy planning must become a priority. You can't just pass money down without a plan. If you do, many errors can occur. But, they don't have to happen to you or your kids. And, you don't have to take on the "second job" of learning how to be financial planner, estate attorney or tax accountant. The process is quite simple. It starts by asking yourself some questions and spending some time really considering your answers.

**Is the family financial legacy important to you?**

**Do you feel you have a firm grasp of the tax liabilities associated with any inheritance you intend to pass on to your children or grandchildren?**

**In other words, what will your kids really inherit – your legacy or liabilities?**

Now, please continue reading.

# Chapter 2

## Economic Trends: Do you have blinders on?

When making financial decisions it is important not to have "blinders" on. You must be generally aware of what is going on politically and economically. Not to say you should be able to debate with a great economist, but you need to have a general sense of what is going on.

This chapter will highlight for you some of the trends that are important to watch and the effects they will have on your income taxes, standard of living, and finances in general. This information is also intended to prompt you to consider how all of this will affect your children and grandchildren.

As you read, please keep in mind that the purpose of this chapter is not to scare you; it is simply to make you aware of the most significant current economic trends.

Entitlement programs are becoming very expensive for the United States to maintain. These programs, which include Medicare, Medicaid, Social Security, and Pensions, are dangerously underfunded and will fail if major changes aren't made.

In fiscal year 2011, Medicare and Medicaid had cost the government $835 billion…23% of U.S. federal spending. The $38.6 trillion in unfunded benefits Medicare is expected to pay over the next 75 years equals $328,404.43 for each of the 117,538,000 households the Census Bureau said there were in the United States in 2010.

"From the 75-year budget perspective, the present value of the additional resources that would be necessary to meet projected expenditures, at current-law levels for the three programs combined, is $38.6 trillion. To put this very large figure in perspective, it would represent 4.3 percent of the present value of projected GDP over the same period ($907 trillion)," [**Source:** 2011 Annual Report of the Boards of Trustees of the Federal Hospital Insurance and Federal Supplementary Medical Insurance Trust Funds]

According to the *USA Today* [6-7-2011; "Government's Mountain of Debt"], "The federal government makes its pension fund contributions with IOUs. Unlike private and state pensions, the federal government does not have a stash of stocks, bonds and other assets to pay future costs. Civil servant retirements will be financed by taxes or borrowing. The unfunded liability for federal pensions is $1.6 trillion, plus another $400 billion for retiree health care. The federal government employs about 2 million people, excluding the military and postal service."

As Baby Boomers enter retirement and live longer, there will be an incredible strain on all government programs. Some of the "fixes" to these problems will be making you wait longer to receive benefits, a reduction of benefit, or possibly the government will have to raise tax revenues to help patch these shortfalls. This is nothing new ... in fact, if you read your Social Security statement you will read that it will be exhausted in 2036. In short, the foundation for which the entitlement programs are built on are crumbling, and in need of major corrections.

## National Debt

It's important to pay attention to our national debt. It's out of control and will have a significant effect on generations to come.

Total interest on the national debt in fiscal 2010 was approx. $395 billion dollars! Think about $395,000,000,000 ... in one dollar bills, its weight is equivalent to 2,220 full-grown blue whales. This is an incredible amount of interest to pay per year. If the government doesn't start to balance their budget, this problem will continue to escalate. What happens when interest rates rise? What will this do to the dollar?

The global economy is on thin ice right now and the U.S. is playing a part in that, which is why the U.S. debt is being watched closely by the global economy.

On August 18th, 2011, the U.S. was downgraded by Moody, which reflected the S&P's "opinion that the fiscal consolidation plan that Congress and the administration recently agreed to falls short of what, in our view, would be necessary to stabilize the government's medium-term debt dynamics."

In 2011, the U.S. government was scrambling around, down to the last minute, to raise the debt ceiling. This allowed the government to print more money to pay the interest on what it already owed. That is like paying your credit card minimum payment with another credit card. Who would advise that?

Yet, if the government had not raised the debt ceiling, the U.S. would not have been able to make their interest payment obligations. So, the government threw a band-aid on the gaping wound. Now they are back to printing money… and everything is great!

The United States of America is the greatest country in the world, and also the only country that is allowed to print as much money as desired because the U.S.A. owns the reserve currency – the dollar. They have no need to balance the budget as long as they can print more money.

However, if the U.S. loses the dollar as the worldwide reserve currency, the government will no longer be able to be a "money factory" and print money whenever it is needed. This would further devalue the dollar and instantly decrease your standard of living by 25-30%. The mountainous debt that was built up over many years will be on the backs of your children and grandchildren.

# Table S–5. Proposed Budget by Category (In billions of dollars)

|  | 2011 | 2012 | 2013 | 2014 | 2015 |
|---|---|---|---|---|---|
| **Outlays:** | | | | | |
| Appropriated ("discretionary") programs: [1] | | | | | |
|   Security | 838 | 868 | 851 | 768 | 749 |
|   Nonsecurity | 462 | 450 | 410 | 393 | 385 |
|     Subtotal, appropriated programs | 1,300 | 1,319 | 1,261 | 1,160 | 1,135 |
| Mandatory programs: | | | | | |
|   Social Security | 725 | 773 | 820 | 867 | 918 |
|   Medicare | 480 | 478 | 523 | 551 | 569 |
|   Medicaid | 275 | 255 | 283 | 338 | 370 |
|   Troubled Asset Relief Program (TARP)[2] | –38 | 35 | 12 | 8 | 5 |
|   Other mandatory programs | 631 | 711 | 654 | 644 | 665 |
|     Subtotal, mandatory programs | 2,073 | 2,252 | 2,293 | 2,409 | 2,527 |
| Net interest | 230 | 225 | 248 | 309 | 390 |
| Adjustments for disaster costs [3] | * | * | 2 | 5 | 7 |
|     Total outlays | 3,603 | 3,796 | 3,803 | 3,883 | 4,060 |
| **Receipts:** | | | | | |
| Individual income taxes | 1,091 | 1,165 | 1,359 | 1,476 | 1,617 |
| Corporation income taxes | 181 | 237 | 348 | 430 | 445 |
| Social insurance and retirement receipts: | | | | | |
|   Social Security payroll taxes | 566 | 572 | 677 | 742 | 781 |
|   Medicare payroll taxes | 188 | 203 | 214 | 226 | 240 |
|   Unemployment insurance | 56 | 57 | 58 | 59 | 75 |
|   Other retirement | 8 | 9 | 10 | 11 | 12 |
| Excise taxes | 72 | 79 | 88 | 99 | 104 |
| Estate and gift taxes | 7 | 11 | 13 | 23 | 25 |
| Customs duties | 30 | 31 | 33 | 36 | 38 |
| Deposits of earnings, Federal Reserve System | 83 | 81 | 80 | 61 | 46 |
| Other miscellaneous receipts | 20 | 24 | 21 | 52 | 68 |
|     Total receipts | 2,303 | 2,469 | 2,902 | 3,215 | 3,450 |
| **Deficit** | 1,300 | 1,327 | 901 | 668 | 610 |
| Net interest | 230 | 225 | 248 | 309 | 390 |
| **Primary deficit / surplus (–)** | 1,070 | 1,102 | 654 | 359 | 219 |
| On-budget deficit | 1,367 | 1,394 | 945 | 695 | 629 |
| Off-budget deficit / surplus (–) | –67 | –67 | –43 | –27 | –19 |
| **Memorandum, budget authority for appropriated programs:** [1] | | | | | |
|   Security | 847 | 817 | 788 | 743 | 756 |
|   Nonsecurity | 370 | 379 | 359 | 366 | 373 |
|     Total, appropriated funding | 1,217 | 1,195 | 1,147 | 1,108 | 1,129 |

\* $500 million or less.

1 Discretionary spending levels other than Overseas Contingency Operations reflect the budget authority caps under the Budget Control Act of 2011. The split of discretionary spending between security and nonsecurity after 2013 is based on increasing budget authority in each category by the growth rate in the aggregate discretionary cap.

2 Outlays for TARP result from obligations incurred through October 3, 2010 for the Home Affordable Modification Program and other TARP programs.

Source: U.S. Government; whitehouse.org

| 2016 | 2017 | 2018 | 2019 | 2020 | 2021 | 2022 | 2013-2017 | 2013-2022 |
|---|---|---|---|---|---|---|---|---|
| 757 | 771 | 786 | 803 | 820 | 837 | 856 | 3,897 | 8,001 |
| 386 | 390 | 397 | 405 | 415 | 420 | 430 | 1,964 | 4,032 |
| **1,143** | **1,162** | **1,183** | **1,208** | **1,236** | **1,258** | **1,287** | **5,861** | **12,033** |
| 970 | 1,026 | 1,085 | 1,149 | 1,216 | 1,287 | 1,361 | 4,601 | 10,699 |
| 619 | 633 | 654 | 716 | 767 | 822 | 908 | 2,895 | 6,762 |
| 399 | 423 | 450 | 479 | 510 | 542 | 578 | 1,813 | 4,372 |
| 2 | 1 | * | * | * | ........ | ........ | 29 | 30 |
| 705 | 712 | 716 | 750 | 775 | 821 | 826 | 3,381 | 7,269 |
| **2,695** | **2,796** | **2,905** | **3,094** | **3,269** | **3,472** | **3,673** | **12,719** | **29,131** |
| 483 | 565 | 631 | 692 | 748 | 798 | 850 | 1,996 | 5,715 |
| 8 | 9 | 9 | 10 | 10 | 10 | 10 | 31 | 80 |
| **4,329** | **4,532** | **4,728** | **5,004** | **5,262** | **5,537** | **5,820** | **20,607** | **46,959** |
| 1,763 | 1,912 | 2,052 | 2,184 | 2,319 | 2,459 | 2,605 | 8,128 | 19,747 |
| 455 | 473 | 480 | 485 | 494 | 507 | 520 | 2,151 | 4,637 |
| 833 | 881 | 936 | 987 | 1,034 | 1,093 | 1,150 | 3,915 | 9,113 |
| 257 | 273 | 290 | 306 | 321 | 339 | 357 | 1,210 | 2,823 |
| 79 | 75 | 73 | 65 | 64 | 66 | 67 | 347 | 681 |
| 12 | 13 | 13 | 14 | 14 | 16 | 17 | 57 | 130 |
| 106 | 112 | 120 | 136 | 142 | 150 | 159 | 509 | 1,216 |
| 27 | 29 | 32 | 34 | 37 | 39 | 42 | 117 | 301 |
| 39 | 41 | 44 | 46 | 48 | 50 | 52 | 188 | 428 |
| 36 | 36 | 38 | 40 | 42 | 43 | 45 | 260 | 468 |
| 71 | 74 | 77 | 83 | 89 | 95 | 101 | 286 | 729 |
| **3,680** | **3,919** | **4,153** | **4,379** | **4,604** | **4,857** | **5,115** | **17,167** | **40,274** |
| **649** | **612** | **575** | **626** | **658** | **681** | **704** | **3,440** | **6,684** |
| 483 | 565 | 631 | 692 | 748 | 798 | 850 | 1,996 | 5,715 |
| 166 | 47 | −56 | −67 | −90 | −117 | −146 | 1,445 | 969 |
| 673 | 634 | 601 | 647 | 667 | 686 | 701 | 3,576 | 6,877 |
| −24 | −22 | −25 | −21 | −10 | −5 | 4 | −136 | −193 |
| 769 | 785 | 802 | 819 | 836 | 853 | 874 | 3,841 | 8,023 |
| 381 | 389 | 398 | 407 | 416 | 425 | 435 | 1,867 | 3,947 |
| **1,150** | **1,174** | **1,199** | **1,225** | **1,251** | **1,277** | **1,309** | **5,708** | **11,970** |

3 These amounts represent a placeholder for major disasters requiring Federal assistance for relief and reconstruction. Such assistance might be provided in the form of discretionary or mandatory outlays or tax relief. These amounts are included as outlays for convenience.

Income taxes were originally enacted in 1862 to support the Civil War. Throughout the late 19th century and early 20th century, the income tax evolved and, with the passing of the 16th Amendment to the Constitution in 1913, it has morphed into a complicated tax code to fund all sorts of govern-ment programs, agencies and entitlements as shown earlier in this Chapter.

Your financial future is directly tied to current and projected tax revenue. Take a look at the ***Proposed Budget of the U.S. Fiscal Year 2013*** (shown on previous page). There is some very interesting infor-mation in it. The federal government is estimating individual federal income tax revenues of $1.165 trillion in 2012. In 2020, they are estimating 2.319 trillion dollars. They have built their budget based on almost doubling individual federal income tax reven-ues in the next few years.

Where will this extra tax revenue come from, especially in light of the fact that unemployment is over 9%, with about 19% under-employed, as of this writing?

And, what happens to the budget if these tax revenues don't come through?

Most likely, there will be an increase in income taxes. But, believe it or not, here's some good news. This is the one area that you actually have some control over as far as protecting yourself. So, please pay attention because understanding your tax obligations, and making tax planning a priority, are two ways you can protect yourself.

Most people spend a couple hours each year gathering their information for their tax returns, usually a few weeks or days before they are due. And then, they are so relieved it's done, they give very little thought to the issue until the next year. This is referred to as "reactive accounting", which means making tax decisions today, without looking into the future. You need to look to the future and make tax planning more important to you throughout the year, not just in April.

## Economic Trends: Do you have blinders on?

Think about how taxes affect your income. Then, think back to the scenario presented in Chapter 1 and think about how taxes affect inheritances. It's very clear that increased income taxes will further erode the value of tax-deferred investments.

Look at it this way: Let's say you have a $100,000 IRA. At a 20% tax-bracket, you really only have $80K. Now let's say taxes go to 40%. Now your IRA is only worth $60K.

Take a look at this graph. It represents the progression of income taxes since the passing of the 16th Amendment (1913) which made income tax a permanent aspect of the U.S. taxpayer system. Very quickly, income taxes became such a boon to the government's coffers that the government then said, "Wow! This is fun! Let's tax the public some more so we can build stuff and get bigger."

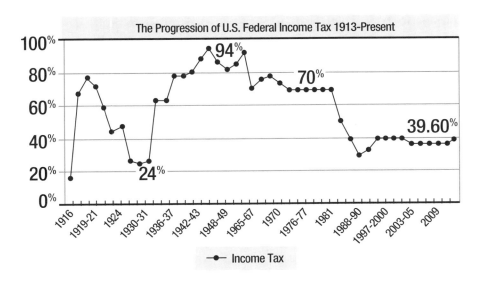

Notice the protracted period of time between the 1930's through the 80's. During that 50+ year timeframe, the top tax bracket remained over 60%! Can you imagine if you made a dollar and only got sixty cents in return after taxes? A 60-70% tax rate means that some individuals, after state and federal income tax, may only get thirty or forty cents for every dollar they make; it kind of suppresses the urge to make a great deal of money, doesn't it?

## The Tax Implications of Your Investments

Since the inception of the 401(K) which occurred in 1981, income taxes have been at a historic low yet the government has always been the strongest advocate of 401(K)s and has made great efforts to tell us it would be better to put our money into tax-qualified plans for retirement. In fact, the government wanted *all employees* to automatically be enrolled into one of these plans with 3% of their earnings going into it and suggested that an employee would have to opt-out to not participate.

Why do they want us to contribute to these plans so badly?

Think about it this way. Which would you rather be taxed on – the seed (your original amount of investment) or the harvest (your investments after they've grown over time)? Naturally, like any farmer, you would rather be taxed on your seeds. But, the government recognizes it's better to tax you on your harvest.

## It's Your Decision

You may think proper diversification of your investments means to own a variety of mutual funds, stocks, annuities, bonds, large-cap, small-cap, and international funds. This may be fine from an asset allocation standpoint. But, have any of the financial professionals you may have consulted with over the years ever shown you how each type of investment will be taxed?

Keep in mind, you take on all the risk in the investment yet, you may have to give half of your return to Uncle Sam. Uncle Sam didn't take any risk on the downside (when you invested your money), yet gets fully "rewarded" on your upside (when your investment makes more money). It is likely that with some investments, you took on all the risk only to give up a considerable amount of your reward to taxes. Simply put, you can reap more revenue from your investments if you pay attention to how they are taxed.

Based on the national debt, it seems inevitable that taxes will go up in the near future, though there is much debate on how the government is going to do it. A lot of discussion centers on increasing the tax liability on people who make over $250,000 a year. Yet, other discussions lean toward simplifying the tax code or installing a flat tax for everyone. In any case, almost everyone agrees that reducing government spending will help ease the tax burden, but it won't solve the problem.

Formulate your own opinions and decide for yourself if we are living in dangerous and uncertain financial times. But, keep in mind that the decisions you make today can make a large difference to your family in the future. The events that have transpired over the last few decades, coupled with this current economy, will not only affect the quality of your retirement and the way you will pass money down to the next generation, but will also have an impact on your financial legacy for generations to come.

Take a moment and think about how taxes will affect your retirement and investment income. If they go up, your rate of return on your investments – 401(K)s, IRAs, and other tax deferred accounts – will be lower because they will be taxed at a higher rate.

These types of investments are the vehicles in which many people have a majority of their money. Are you one of them? If so, it is important to understand that relying solely on these vehicles can only guarantee you one thing – that you will likely transfer significant portions of your wealth to the government, unknowingly and unnecessarily.

With that in mind, it's time to ask yourself some more questions.

**Are your blinders off? Do you see how current economic trends could affect your children, grandchildren, and your financial legacy?**

**Based on the information presented in this Chapter, do you believe income taxes will increase in the future?**

**Do you feel it is worthwhile to consider making adjustments to your financial plan and talking to a financial professional who can help you make the changes that are needed?**

Now, please read on. The next couple Chapters will examine what you can do today that will help position your family to be a step ahead in years to come; not that you intend to make them "rich," but to live the same quality of lifestyle that you were afforded.

# Chapter 3

## Is the Family Legacy Important to You?

You have lived a long and fruitful life. How will you be remembered? Or, how do you want to be remembered?

This answer will be different for everyone. You'll be more likely to arrive at a true answer for yourself if you understand that the family legacy captures the history, culture, experience, values and aspirations of a collective family and its members over time.

A family legacy expresses where the family has come from as well as where they are headed together. This legacy also encompasses faith, love, traditions, morals, and wealth. If you have a family, you have been blessed in many ways. If you have children, you have likely helped guide them through life; now they are grown and have their own families. Perhaps your life enables you ample time to spend with your grandchildren, who are precious to you and bring you much joy.

These are all great things that have helped to shape your family legacy. But, in addition to the "emotional" aspect, you must tend to the financial portion of your legacy.

There are really two ways to pass down a financial legacy. One way is through the financial discipline and strategies, i.e., the money management and financial "culture", your family instilled and practiced. The other is money.

Combining these two methods is the most effective way to help build and sustain wealth within the family. Think about it this way. What is the point of passing down money if there is no discipline or "culture" established for how to manage the money?

Sadly, people don't seem to talk about their finances anymore. It is as if finances, whether it's "money troubles" or money management, are deemed "private" or none of anybody's business! But, it is very important for families to discuss finances. There is no point in holding the family financial cards close to your chest.

Yet, this is how many people transfer their wealth and this disconnect is causing much ruin in today's society. It is imperative that parents discuss finances with their children. As a parent, you have much guidance to offer your kids; if they don't get it at home, where else will they get it? If you're not sure about your qualifications as your kids' financial advisor, just think about the financial "do-overs" you would have done throughout your life, had you been able to.

Like everyone, you've probably made financial mistakes, missteps, or "bad bets". If you compile those mistakes and add them up, what is the total? (Don't forget to include opportunity costs.) Now, if you could go back, recover the money you lost through mistakes and missteps - at the time you made them - and had put the money in your bank account earning interest instead, how much more money would you have today?

One of the definitions of insanity is doing the same thing over and over again and expecting different results. ***You want to make sure your children don't make the same financial mistakes you have made in the past.*** Please slow down for a second and let that sink in. You want to make sure your children don't make the same financial mistakes you have made in the past. This is the main point of the financial legacy. Share your wealth and wisdom, as well as your mistakes.

Having financial discussions with your family allows you to create an open forum. You can share information freely which helps foster a strong family enterprise. Your children will still make mistakes but maybe you can save them from some of the bear traps you stepped into. Having these discussions also allows you to tell your children what is important to you when you are no longer here. Maybe it is important that they use the money you intend to leave them for the grandchildren's college education, or for their retirement. It doesn't matter what the money is for, but this gives you the opportunity to discuss your wishes.

By having these discussions now, it will make it much easier for your children to cooperate with each other as they close out the estate and divide the assets after you pass away. Many times these conversations never happen and families fight over who gets what, which can ultimately ruin the family relationship.

If you manage these conversations patiently and rationally and remind your kids of their true purpose, they can be very productive; not to mention that being involved in your kids' inheritance while you are alive allows you to preempt or prevent tension or arguments after you are gone.

Candid financial discussions cannot resolve every issue between your kids or grandkids, but they sure can help. They can leave a lasting impact that can strengthen your family's position. These discussions don't have to be about how much money you have in the bank. They can be about the economy, how money works, the importance of hard work, and the socio-economic history of the family.

As Chapter 2 pointed out, it is more important than ever to try to ensure that your children and grandchildren will have a much different retirement experience than you. Pensions are a thing of the past. Social Security and Medicare are failing. It can easily cost $100,000 to send a child to college. Today, families will have to work much harder and longer to get ahead.

## The Family as an Enterprise

Think about the family enterprise. Let's look at a typical example. You have a good retirement portfolio and some extra money. You go down to the local bank and walk up to the counter and tell the person you want to put $50,000 into a CD. It is set up for you at 1% interest. The bank then takes that money and turns it into a loan. Your child walks into the bank to get a new car loan which is offered at 6%. They are paying you 1% and then charging your child 6%. This is one of the ways banks make their profit. So why can't you do this yourself? Everyone's situation is different, but family banking is one example of how a family increases its wealth.

Then there is money. Most work really hard to earn and save it, then have a hard time spending it because spending money instead of accumulating it is against their nature. In other words, many people in retirement have become hard-wired to hanging onto money and can't "reprogram" themselves into feeling comfortable letting go of it.

Are you in your 70's and 80's with many accumulated assets? This is commendable but also a place for careful thought. First, if you haven't yet done so, give yourself permission to spend your money, not foolishly, of course, but you are entitled to live as enjoyably as you are able. Then, determine how to pass your assets to the next generation efficiently and painlessly, as you desire.

Passing money (your financial legacy) down to the next generation may be one of the greatest gifts you can give to your family. Being so important, this gift must be "wrapped" in thoughtful, deliberate planning so it is maximized.

## Is the Family Legacy Important to You?

This is exactly what Royalty (those born into monarchies), colleges, nonprofits, and the wealthiest do every day. Royalty has passed down their jewels, real estate, castles, and significant wealth for decades and centuries; it took generations to accumulate the wealth and treasures many royal families have enjoyed, and still enjoy. Regardless, each generation of a royal family comes into the world with wealth and assets. Some generations contributed to the wealth, thereby increasing it for the next generation, some didn't.

Colleges and nonprofits operate in a similar manner. They have endowments. People have been donating and leaving money to some Colleges and Universities for hundreds of years. These institutions have always been smart with the endowment funds and how they have been invested. Harvard's endowment recently reached $32 billion. But Harvard did not start with this type of money; it was accumulated over 300+ years.

The wealthiest in the country also build endowments for their family. They accumulate all of their life, make sure their retirement is taken care of, and then prioritize the legacy they will leave their children. This gives the next generation an advantage as they embark into the world. They can leverage their endowment by using it to buy a business, go to the most prestigious universities, or create residual investment income.

Wealth-building in the family needs to start somewhere and you don't need to be ultra-wealthy in order to be the "pioneer". Passing down money, financial discipline and wisdom can have a huge effect, no matter the amount or extent. Remember, if your family financial legacy is set up correctly, you can leave a footprint for many generations to come. Your starting point is determining if your family legacy is important to you; if it is, then please take a moment to ask yourself some questions that pertain to what will happen after you have passed away.

**Do you want to give the next generation of your family an advantage?**

**If you did leave your kids and grandkids a significant financial sum as an inheritance, would they manage it wisely or foolishly?**

**Does this concern you?**

Now, please continue reading.

# Chapter 4

## What is Your Exit Strategy?

If you are retired, or see it on your horizon, you have likely worked hard all of your life. You've had some great times and some tough times; some rough patches and some smooth patches. Like most Americans, you and/or your spouse probably enjoyed a good career, watched your children grow up, and had the opportunity to pursue a passion or two along the way.

Simply put, reaching retirement is a lifelong journey; yet, its destination is often greeted with "Now what?" followed by a few concerns. The first and main concern is retirement income; the second concern is health care costs, and the third concern pertains to your children and grandchildren, in particular, the current economic strains reminiscent of the Great Depression era that they will be subjected to.

Let's take a realistic look at each one of these concerns in more detail.

### Retirement Income

Many retirees have a difficult time adjusting to retirement. During the working years, when in the "accumulation stage" of life, saving money and taking on risk is natural because "time is on your side". But, retirement becomes the "distribution phase". At this point, retirees will either spend all of their money just to live or pass money down to the next generation.

Thus, the main concern in retirement is income. When you retire, you give up your monthly paycheck. But, that income needs to be replaced … somehow.

Most retired individuals collect Social Security. This was paid into through paycheck deductions throughout the wage-earning years to guarantee a regular income after those years have passed. But this income may not be sufficient to take care of living expenses.

Other retirees collect a pension income from their employer. The combination of the two many times is sufficient to cover the standard costs of living. That is why it is so important to determine – in advance – exactly what your monthly expenses, (your cost of living) will be before you retire – regardless of whether you have Social Security and/or a pension.

One way to do that is to sit down with a financial professional who can help you determine how much income is needed. This is a very important and rather simple step in the retirement planning process. First, look at your monthly expenses, which include: mortgage payment, insurance, taxes, food, clothing, gas, car, vacations, utilities, health care (prescriptions, co-pays, and insurance premiums) and discretionary expenses (gifts, for example).

A good source for tracking your actual monthly expenses is the past year's bank statements. Once you determine what your expenses are today, you have to add an inflation factor. For example, the cost of gas today will not be the same in ten years due to inflation.

An important trend to keep in mind when doing your future financial planning and calculating for inflation is that most retirees spend the most money in the first ten years of retirement. Expenses tend to decline in the mid 70's because of a decrease in activity. Most people take fewer and shorter vacations, for example.

Once you have determined your income needs, you have to assess your income sources - before or after taxes. For instance, Social Security can be tax free, but pensions are typically taxable. With your income needs and your "net" income (income after taxes) determined, you'll be able to check and verify if you will have a surplus or a shortfall.

If you have a shortfall between expenses and income, you will have to derive income from your investments. If you're like most retirees, you have saved for years and have money in IRA's, bank accounts, CD's, and other investments. Today, many people are also putting their money into fixed-indexed annuities. These are like "private pensions" and are great if utilized properly. They offer income riders that allow you to draw 5-7% for your lifetime.

For example, if you put $100K in a fixed-indexed annuity, you can draw $5000-$7000 per year for the rest of your life – regardless of what the stock market is doing. It is money you can't outlive; it will pay regardless of your age, or how long you live. Fixed-indexed annuities also offer preservation of capital, meaning you can't lose money. In these volatile markets, this peace of mind can help you really enjoy retirement.

After sitting down with a financial professional and completing an income plan, many retirees discover they will have extra money after all monthly expenses are covered. The key is to save properly. If you have saved properly, you do not need to take risk in retirement. You can enter into it with a different mindset, and experience it with a sense of security. And remember, the monies you saved throughout your accumulation years were saved to spend in retirement, so enjoy them!

## Health Care

Health care prices are always rising. This is quite daunting to someone who'll be living another twenty to thirty years on an income that will likely not rise at the same rate as the costs to maintain their health and wellness. As a retiree gets older, health care needs and costs increase;

these costs can range from $1000 to $12,000 per month, which can eat through income quickly.

Health care prices have been growing at a staggering pace over the last few years. Group health insurance prices have been going up over 20% per year. It is well known that these costs are getting out of control. If you are retiring before you are 65 you must keep this in mind. People in their 60's will pay $500-$1000 per month per individual, depending on coverage. At the age of 65, most are eligible for Medicare.

There is no cost to Medicare Part A, which is hospital insurance that helps cover in-patient care in hospitals, skilled nursing facility, hospice, and home health care. However, once enrolled in Medicare Part B which helps cover medically-necessary services like doctors' services, outpatient care, durable medical equipment, home health services, and other medical services and some preventative services, this premium is deducted from your Social Security check.

In 2011, the Medicare Part B premium was $96.40 per month. In addition, many retirees are taking out a Medicare supplement that fills in the gaps of the plan and provides prescription drug coverage. All in, you may be spending $300 per month. And, if you are taking monthly prescriptions, or need medical tests or certain procedures, you may incur additional costs, which will continue to inflate.

Another major medical cost some people have to undertake is for assisted living. According to Social Security's actuarial table, a 65 year old male will live an average of 17.19 more years. As people live longer, there is a higher probability that they may need assistance in their later years. Some will stay in their home, but still need help with things like cooking, cleaning, bathing, transferring (mobility assistance in and out of the home), errands, transportation to and from appointments, or grocery shopping. You may be fortunate and have family that can help you with this; if not, you will need to pay someone for these services.

Some retirees will need this type of help and medical care or may need to move into an assisted living facility or nursing home. These types of facilities could cost anywhere from $3000-$12,000 per month depending on the facility and the type of care received. Have you thought about what would happen to your retirement if this were to happen? How well off would this leave your surviving spouse? These are things that should be considered. While there is insurance you can purchase to protect you from some or all of these risks, this is the one area that could drastically affect your retirement lifestyle.

## The Next Generation

Lastly, many retirees worry about the next generation. Chapter 2 presented this issue with a discussion of some economic trends. What is happening now will impact future generations and make it harder for them to get ahead. If you have the ability to help your children and grandchildren, do you want to maximize it?

The first thing that ALL retirees should do is get their legal work in order. This means sitting down with an attorney and putting in place a will, trusts, medical power of attorney, and financial power of attorney.

A will is the most basic part of estate plan. This is where you can state your final wishes. A will is looked at in Probate court by the judge. Most people however want to avoid Probate court. When you pass away, unless you set them up properly, your assets will go to Probate court, which can get very expensive and take weeks to months to years to resolve. And, during that time, your family will not have access to your assets; they will be frozen. In addition, there will be a notice in the newspaper letting people know you passed away. This notice will also list all of your assets for the public to see. This is when people and family come out of the woodwork and try to collect their share.

This should be particularly concerning to those who are on their second or third marriages. If you are divorced, your assets could get dispersed in ways you would never have authorized. Avoiding Probate is why it is so important to set yourself up properly; the most common way to do this is with a trust.

A trust is really just a piece of paper until you fund it. You will want to work with a lawyer who can help you choose the right trusts according to your needs. Many people draft a revocable trust. With this type of trust you will remain in control of assets, while changing ownership of them to the trust you set up. For example, you can't assign a beneficiary to a house, but it will likely be an asset you will pass down. A revocable trust will define how your house will be inherited, or who the house will be left to so a judge doesn't decide that for you in Probate. [**Note:** There is also an irrevocable trust that is used for larger estates to protect assets from exorbitant tax liabilities, but this discussion focuses strictly on the revocable trust.]

To set up a revocable trust, you first take inventory of all of your assets that don't have beneficiaries. Most commonly, this would be your bank accounts, CD's, house, and non-qualified investment accounts. Chances are that you are the current owner of each of these assets and accounts.

You will need to create the revocable trust first and then fund it by going to the banks where you have accounts and re-titling each one so your trust is now the owner. Then, establish the trustee, the person who will follow your wishes as stated in the trust. Upon your death, your trustee will now have access to the trust and have immediate access to the bank accounts. By doing this, you have made it convenient for your designated person to take care of the expenses that come flooding in at this distressing time.

The medical and financial power of attorney is also very important. This allows your designated person to make financial and medical decisions for you in times when you can't make these decisions for yourself. You can lay out your wishes for this person to honor.

## What is Your Exit Strategy?

Once you have all of the legal work complete, you will need to look at your assets with a financial professional. Many retirees will have multiple accounts or assets. Let's look at the purpose of each asset and how it will pass down to the next generation.

### *IRAs*

Most retirees have an IRA. During your working years you were always told that you need to save money for retirement. Most people have saved a majority of their retirement money in their company's retirement plan. Once you retire, you roll your 401(K) into your own personal IRA. Reminder: These monies were deposited into the account before you paid taxes. When you take money out of your IRA, it is all income taxable. At age 70½ you will need to take your RMD or required minimum distribution. If you don't take RMD you will be penalized by the IRS.

It is important to look at this account and categorize it. Is this money that you will need for income or will it be part of your legacy? If you don't need to rely on it for income, then it's important for you to look at the account. If you believe income taxes are going up, does it make sense to defer taxes to a future date when they may be higher?

If your IRA will be part of your financial legacy, you need to know that most inheritances are spent in the first 2½ months. Most people who inherit money in this economy spend it quickly. They pay off credit cards, buy a new house, put in a new kitchen, buy a new car, go on a nice vacation, and go shopping.

When an IRA is inherited, the way the money is dispersed can make a huge difference. The "Stretch IRA" is one way to disperse it. In this case, your family will keep the IRA and take the RMD's out every year. It is important to set up your beneficiaries properly for this. Keep in mind, maximizing this strategy limits your family's access to the money. One major problem with the "Stretch IRA" is liquidity, especially in light of that fact that, as mentioned above, most people who inherit money spend all of it very soon after receiving it. This behavior presents a real problem – after the fact.

When money is taken out of the IRA, it is ALL taxable, which means taxes will consume an inheritance unless it is set up properly. When the family spends the IRA, it will likely put them in a higher tax bracket. If they are in a higher tax bracket than you were, some of their inheritance will go straight to the IRS, which was probably not your intention. This problem only compounds if taxes go up in the future.

## Bank Accounts and CDs

Everyone has savings and checking accounts. Some may even have a CD with a bank. These accounts are very important components of your financial plan. They offer liquidity for day to day expenses or for various "unscheduled" and unavoidable expenses like new brakes for the car, a leaky roof, or a root canal. The problem with these accounts is low interest rates. You may get one or two percent interest that is taxable. It would take you 72 years to double your money at 1% interest assuming no taxes. While this money is liquid, it loses its purchasing power to inflation every day.

## Property and Real Estate

You may own a home or land. This is one of the largest assets most people own. Commonly, people will have their house paid off in retirement. What do you think happens to your house when you pass away? Your family goes down to the local hardware store and purchases a "For Sale" sign. Your children are grown now and typically already have their own home and children. The house is one of the most ill-liquid assets to pass down to the next generation; significant wealth can be lost. The children and grandchildren may have to carry the costs of the house for months until they sell it. So, in many cases, the family will take a dramatically lower offer on the house just to get rid of it.

## Stocks and Mutual Funds

Many people will own mutual funds and stocks, which are amongst the most volatile types of investments. You will also pay taxes on your gains every year with mutual funds. Even though these investments typically get good returns over the long run, they need to be managed. Buy-hold strategy may not perform well in these markets.

Again, it is important to determine if these investments are going to be used for income or to be passed to the next generation. If you DON'T need these accounts for income you may want to examine their purpose.

Remember, most inheritances are spent in the first 2½ months. If you pass down stock, where will the market be? Many times the heirs won't even pay attention if the market is up or down. They just want access to the money. Imagine if we see another 2008 and you pass away during this time. It could be the worst time to sell the investments. You don't have a crystal ball so you want to make sure you position your money for good growth, but in ways so that the stock market can't affect it.

In summary, it is extremely important that you have an understanding of your retirement income and expenses. Don't be afraid to "crunch the numbers." Many times people realize they will have excess money after completing their retirement income plan. If it turns out that you will also have "left-over " money, it is important for you to allocate it wisely and to avoid taking unnecessary risks.

This is what is meant by your exit strategy. So, before you read on, ask yourself these questions to help you devise one that will see you comfortably through retirement and assure that your financial legacy is passed down exactly as you desire.

**Is it important for you to make sure all of your legal work is complete?**

**Do you have a list of your assets? Have you identified the purpose of each one – currently and as part of your legacy?**

Now, please continue.

# Chapter 5

## Can You Relate to This?

Sometimes it is helpful to hear or read about others' situations in order to better understand what to do about your own. That is the purpose of this Chapter. Even though everyone's situation is unique, there are commonalities. The case studies you will read are about three different individuals with quite common circumstances. As you read, pay attention to things that you may relate to; jot down any questions or notes that you may think of and share them with your financial professional. Remember these are not recommendations; they are realistic fictional "stories" for example only.

### Mr. and Mrs. G.

After 30 years as a state employee, Mr. G. is retired. He is 67 and is in good health. He retired with a good benefit package which includes health care and a pension. During his working years, he accumulated some money that he had saved in the retirement program.

Mrs. G. is a 70 year old retired teacher. Throughout the 30 years that she taught children, she had funded a 403b; she also has a pension. Mr. and Mrs. G's main concerns when entering retirement were income, future health care costs, and leaving a legacy to their three children. Let's look at each one.

They both have pensions and social security. This gives them a total income of $7,500 a month. They own their home and don't have a mortgage anymore. Their monthly expenses are around $5,000 a month. Their fixed income (social security and pensions) are enough to take care of their monthly living expenses. Consequently, even though this year will be the first year that Mrs. G. will have to take her RMD (Required Minimum Distribution) out of her retirement account, she doesn't need this money for income.

They have $50K in a bank account, $100K in CDs, and $300K in combined retirement funds. They have no life or long-term care insurance. They have also not created their trust and will.

As they looked at their financial picture, it was determined that the major factor that could affect their income and quality of daily life would be health care costs. If one of them had a medical or physical setback, their income would be drained quickly.

Based on these facts, what actions do they need to take?

First is the need for the trust and will. The legal work must be in order. Otherwise, their legacy to their children will end up in Probate court.

The next thing they need to assess is their income. Their income needs are 100% met by their guaranteed income sources. But, what will Mrs. G. do with the RMD she has to take this year? Because their income needs are met, their only other concern was a legacy to the next generation and long term health care costs.

Do you see that the way they were positioned was not the best way for them to alleviate their retirement concerns?

They have a house, bank and CD accounts, and retirement funds. Mr. and Mrs. G believed that income taxes were only going to go up. Since they didn't want to burden their children with a larger than necessary tax liability on their inheritance, they repositioned their retirement accounts to maximize these funds for the family legacy.

They could do this because they weren't going to need to rely on their retirement accounts for income.

Here's what they did: They repositioned their $300K in retirement funds over 7 years into a Maximum Efficient Life Contract (this will be covered in Chapter 6). This way they can pass down $700K to their family on a guaranteed, tax free-basis. This contract was also negotiated to include protection against long-term care. This relieved the couple because they were able to create a legacy for their kids, and protect themselves against a long-term care situation. They successfully resolved their critical retirement concerns.

## Ms. H.

Ms. H. is a 75 year old retired nurse. She has been retired for years now and has a really good understanding of her retirement. Her husband is not in her life anymore and she has three daughters, and four grandchildren. Her expenses are being met by her income from Social Security and a small pension. Her house is paid for and she has around $80K in investments.

Ms. H. had also received a $200K inheritance from her parents from the sale of their house that she had deposited in her local bank. She wanted to preserve this money so she could pass it to her grandchildren upon her death. She had a will and trust, but they were created 20 years ago. Her situation is pretty basic and quite common. She was set well for retirement but needed to tend to her estate planning.

What actions does she need to take?

First, she needs to update her estate planning. Many things have changed since she had originally created her will and trust. Once this is complete, she needs to concentrate on the $200K inheritance she had received which was giving about 1% interest sitting in her savings account. Ms. H. doesn't need this money for income and wants it to go to her grandchildren. In addition, she was paying taxes on this small amount of interest. This money wasn't working very hard for her. In fact, with inflation, this account was losing money.

Ms. H. decided to take this $200K and deposit it into a Maximum Efficient Life Contract. This turned the $200K into $400K that will be given to her family – guaranteed and tax-free – when she passes away. This was a way for her to leverage her $200K and turn it into $400K tax-free that would be given to her grandchildren. This accomplished her goal to leave a risk-free, meaningful legacy to her four grandchildren who will always be thankful for how she impacted the quality of their lives.

## Mr. and Mrs. M.

Mrs. M. is 69 years old; Mr. M. is 71. They have been retired for a while and have a very simple lifestyle. They have three children and three grandchildren whom they love dearly so they sat down with a lawyer and had their estate set up properly.

They were savers and had accumulated $2.3 MM which was spread across different accounts – stocks, mutual funds, cash, and CD's. They had no pension and were collecting Social Security. To cover their monthly income shortfall, they take money from their investments, but their current portfolio puts them at considerable risk.

What do they need to do?

First, before they can plan their legacy, they need to understand their retirement income. They knew they needed around $70K in annual income that they were taking off their stock and mutual fund portfolio.

After a discussion with a financial professional, they discovered they could create the income they desired with no investment risk. They repositioned $1.1MM into a fixed-indexed annuity with an income rider. They were relieved to know that their annual income doubles in this specially designed annuity if they should ever need to go into a long-term care situation. This annuity also allows them to get the income they need for the rest of their life with no market risk.

Mr. and Mrs. M. also feared for their children's and grandchildren's future and wanted to leave as much money as possible to them. Now that their income needs were met, it was time to look at the rest of their money. They had about $1.2MM that was going to be left over if they didn't spend it (which they never would).

They applied to qualify for a Maximum Efficient Life Contract. Upon approval, they deposited $490K into this contract, which was the maximum the insurance company would give them with their qualification rating. With this in place, the insurance company will pay their children and grandchildren $2.1M when they both pass away.

With this plan, the family can relax through retirement without having to worry about their income, their investments losing money, or the inheritance they will leave to the next generation. Turning $490K into $2.1M is a good use of leverage (one dollar doing the work of many). This couple had this opportunity because they took the time to determine the PURPOSE of their different accounts.

As mentioned at the beginning of this Chapter, each of these cases had some commonalities – each person was 65 and older; they had children and grandchildren; they had enough income to meet their expenses; they all had accounts they didn't need to utilize for income. Most of all they loved their families and wanted to make the most of their financial legacy.

**If you took a close look at your income, expenses and accounts with a financial professional, would you also have left over money?**

**Are you interested in learning more about MELCs?**

If so, please read Chapter 6.

# Chapter 6

## Can You Maximize Your Legacy?

Up to this point you have taken a look at the current economy, your family, and the importance of financial planning for your retirement and your legacy. Based on what you have read and hopefully considered so far, have you been able to determine if you will have left over money? Many people do. This is not a bad thing…you just want to maximize it.

In Chapter 5, you were introduced to a solution many people are using for legacy planning – the Maximum Efficient Life Contract. The purpose of this Chapter is to explain the Maximum Efficient Life Contract and show you how to qualify for it.

Using the IRS tax code Section 101 and 7702, you can build yourself a Maximum Efficient Life Contract (MELC). This is a specially designed life insurance contract. This contract can cover an individual or a couple. The main purpose of the MELC is to pass money down to the next generation *tax-free*.

Besides the tax advantages, this contract is one of the only financial tools that utilizes leverage. As mentioned in Chapter 5, leverage, in a financial sense, means to make one dollar do the work of many. These contracts are attractive to many people because they have guarantees. Meaning, you have a contract with an insurance company that will pay off in the future when you pass away.

The insurance company says, "You give me this amount and we will give you this." These contracts can be designed according to your needs. When you are repositioning your assets into a MELC, there is a lot of flexibility. You can design it for a lump sum deposit, five deposits, seven deposits, ten deposits, or you can make deposits every year for the rest of your life. You can design this contract to build up cash value or you can forego use of the money for maximum benefit.

You can design yours by sitting down with a financial professional who is licensed to provide life insurance. In some insurance contracts, you can select a long-term care benefit; meaning, if you went into a long-term care situation, you would have access to your leveraged death benefit to help provide money for this need. With this type of option, you will always receive benefit. If you pass away, your family will get the death benefit tax-free. If you become frail in your older age, it can help pay for care. It is a win-win.

This insurance contract typically offers a 5-9% annual return. This return is the *tax-free* rate if you pass away in your low to mid 80's, depending on how you qualified. This would mean you would have to earn between 7-11% in a taxable account to get the same return the MELC can do on a guaranteed basis. If you live into your 90's, the return will go down to 3-6%. If you live over 100, you may pay into the contract more than it is worth.

Either way, what accounts do you have that will offer you this type of return tax-free?

Because of the potential for returns, these types of contracts have attracted hedge-funds and pensions; they are buying them because they see their value and profitability. There is also a secondary market called life settlement companies that will buy MELCs off people who no longer need or want their insurance. In this market, a company may give a percentage of the death benefit to you up front and when you pass away, they collect the death benefit. Hedge-funds and pensions are spending millions buying these contracts so they must see this as an attractive return on their investment.

This contract has a lot of flexibility, but this isn't important until you qualify. The insurance company may restrict the amount you can put into this contract. They will look at your income, your left over money after expenses, special needs, and your overall net-worth and situation.

Besides being able to qualify financially, you will also have to take a physical and qualify with your health. You should not worry here. Most health conditions are accepted, but there are some that will block you from getting this contract. For example, if you and your doctor are managing usual conditions like high blood pressure or cholesterol, you will not be refused. However, if you had a stroke or a high-stage cancer within a year of applying, you may not be approved.

After going through the underwriting process, you may get an offer that was more or less than what you would have liked. Again, it is important for you to qualify for a MELC before considering it. Try not to get bogged down in the details here; you must first find out if you qualify and for what you have qualified. There is no commitment on your part, so you have nothing to lose by going through the qualification process. A financial professional can help you get approved and help you with the best design for your circumstances.

Once you have been approved and created your design, the last step will be funding the contract. Do you remember Mr. and Mrs. M. from Chapter 5? They turned $490K into $2.1M.

In summary, a MELC is one of the most efficient ways to pass money to the next generation. This contract offers a competitive rate of return, a tax-free benefit, and use of leverage. A MELC also offers a major source of liquidity and takes market timing out of the equation for an inheritance.

# Conclusion

Your legacy can be sustained for generations to come. It is great if you are already set up to leave a legacy to your family. But, in light of current economic trends it is imperative for those of you who are among the aging population, or those of you who will receive some type of financial inheritance, to gain and maintain awareness of how to construct the wisest plans for maximizing your legacy to the next generation.

More than likely, even if you have not planned at all, your family will still inherit something – it could be your house, or perhaps some money. But, if you are not satisfied with that, and if potential tax liabilities or probate court intervention concerns you at all, then it is important that you do a bit more diligence and make an effort to maximize your financial legacy.

Consider exploring a Maximum Efficient Life Contract; there are many ways to fund one. Look at accounts that you won't use. Look at RMDs from your IRAs that you don't need for income. Consider "unwinding" accounts, which means to take money out of accounts that will be taxed at higher rates over an extended period of time to spread tax liability over years. Look at the possibility of leveraging your home equity.

It has been the intent of this book to shine light on the importance of estate planning. Take the time, now, regardless of your current station in life, to look at your situation carefully and utilize every opportunity you have to maximize your estate. If you love your family, make sure you do your best to help them when you are no longer around.

# Glossary

**Annuity:** Any type of payment with a fixed annual payment amount.

**Financial professional:** A certified, trained professional who provides financial services and guidance regarding estate planning, taxes, wills and trusts, and investments.

**Fixed-Indexed Annuity:** A type of annuity that grows at the greater of a) an annual, guaranteed minimum rate of return; or b) the return from a specified stock market index (such as the S&P 500®), reduced by certain expenses and formulas. The returns on fixed-indexed annuities are often similar to CDs, traditional fixed annuities or high grade bonds, but carry the potential for a small hedge against inflation in an up market.

At the time when a fixed-indexed annuity is opened, the number of years until the principal is guaranteed and the surrender period is finished is determined. Even in a down market, a fixed-indexed annuity doesn't ever lose principal (providing that the underlying insurance company stays solvent; to date, no insurance company has ever failed to pay out on a fixed-indexed annuity).

**Income rider:** An irrevocable structured payout of an **annuity** with a specified payment beginning at a specified date, paid at specified intervals over a stated period of months or years or for the duration of the lifetime of the annuitant, potentially his or her spouse, and/or other individuals depending upon the payout option selected.

**Irrevocable trust:** A trust that can't be modified or terminated without the permission of the beneficiary. The grantor, having transferred assets into the trust, effectively removes all of his or her rights of ownership to the assets and the trust.

**Leverage:** In a financial sense, making one dollar do the "work" of many.

**MELC:** Maximum Efficient Life Contract (MELC); a specially designed life insurance contract with the main purpose being to allow a couple or individual to pass money down to the next generation *tax-free*.

**Opportunity Cost:** The cost of any activity measured in terms of the value of the next best alternative that was not chosen. It is the sacrifice (or loss) related to making one choice over several other relative choices.

**Revocable Trust:** A trust whereby provisions can be altered or canceled dependent on the grantor. During the life of the trust, income earned is distributed to the grantor, and only after death does property transfer to the beneficiaries.

**RMD:** Required Minimum Distribution; Individuals with IRAs are required to begin lifetime RMDs from their IRAs no later than April 1 of the year after they reach age 70½. This is in contrast to RMDs from employer-sponsored plans which, in most cases, may be postponed until after the employee retires or reaches age 70½, whichever is later. An individual does not have to take lifetime RMDs from Roth IRAs, but after-death distributions are required.

A person can always withdraw more than the minimum amount from the IRA or plan in any year, but if less than the required amount is withdrawn, the person is subjected to an IRS excise tax equal to 50% of the amount that should have been withdrawn. This penalty is in addition to ordinary income at the individual's marginal rate and any state income taxes.

**Stretch IRA:** An individual retirement arrangement (IRA) set up in a way that extends the period of tax-deferred earnings beyond the lifetime of the owner, typically over several generations. The benefits of "stretching IRA"s can be maximized by leaving as much in the IRA to grow tax-deferred as is legal and by designating beneficiaries who are young enough to exhaust the maximum legal distribution period, defined as the original non-spouse beneficiary's life expectancy.